1937

YEARBOOK

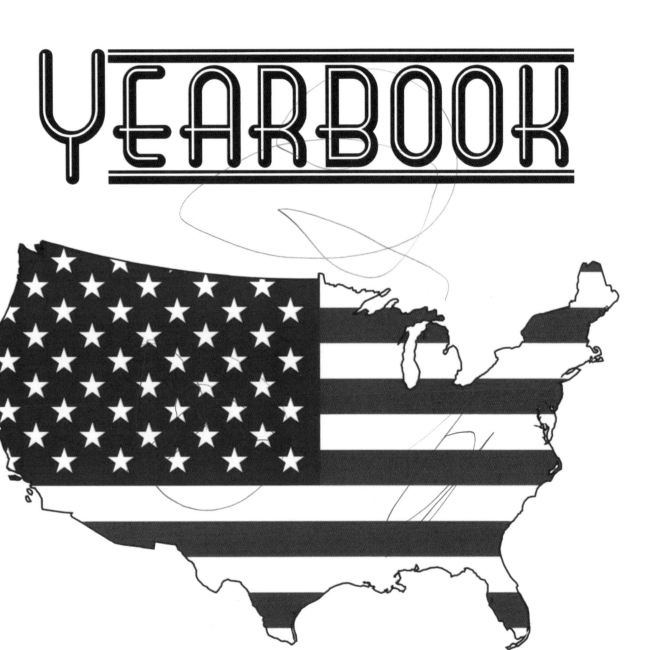

ISBN-10: 1537294784
ISBN-13: 978-1537294780

INDEX

FIRST EDITION

PEOPLE IN HIGH OFFICE

Franklin D. Roosevelt
March 4, 1933 - April 12, 1945
Democratic Party

Born January 30, 1882 and commonly known by his initials FDR he served as the 32nd President of the United States. He died April 12, 1945.

48 stars (1912-1959)

Vice President: John Nance Garner
Chief Justice: Charles Evans Hughes
Speakers of the House of Representatives: William B. Bankhead
Senate Majority Leader: Joseph Taylor Robinson / Alben W. Barkley

UNITED KINGDOM

Monarch - King George VI
Reign: December 11, 1936 - February 6, 1952

Prime Minister Stanley Baldwin
June 7, 1935 - May 28, 1937
Conservative Party

Prime Minister Neville Chamberlain
May 28, 1937 - May 10, 1940
Conservative Party

REST OF THE WORLD

 Argentina — President Agustín Pedro Justo

 Australia — Prime Minister Joseph Lyons

 Brazil — President Getúlio Vargas

 Canada — Prime Minister William Lyon Mackenzie King

 Republic Of China — Premier Chiang Kai-shek

 Cuba — President Federico Laredo Brú

France

President
Albert François Lebrun

Germany

Chancellor
Adolf Hitler

Greece

Prime Minister
Ioannis Metaxas

India

Governor General / Viceroy Of India
Victor Alexander John Hope

Ireland

Head Of Government
Éamon de Valera

Italy

Prime Minister
Benito Mussolini

Japan

Prime Ministers
Kōki Hirota
Senjūrō Hayashi
Prince Fumimaro Konoe

Mexico

President
Lázaro Cárdenas

New Zealand

Prime Minister
Michael Joseph Savage

Portugal

Premier
António de Oliveira Salazar

South Africa

Prime Minister
J. B. M. Hertzog

Soviet Union

Communist Party Leader
Joseph Stalin

Spain

President
Manuel Azaña

Turkey

Prime Ministers
İsmet İnönü
Celâl Bayar

EVENTS FROM 1937

JANUARY

11	The first issue of Look magazine goes on sale.
12	Adventurer and filmmaker Martin Johnson, of Martin and Osa Johnson fame, is killed along with four others in the crash of Western Air Express Flight 7 in mountainous terrain near Saugus, California.
19	Howard Hughes sets a new record flying from Los Angeles to New York City.
20	Chief Justice Charles Evans Hughes swears in Franklin D. Roosevelt for a second term. This is the first time Inauguration Day in the United States occurs on this date, in response to the ratification in 1933 of the 20th amendment to the U.S. Constitution. Inauguration has occurred on January 20 ever since.
26	Michigan celebrates its Centennial Anniversary of statehood.
31	The Ohio River floods. With damage stretching from Pittsburgh to Cairo, Illinois, one million people were left homeless, 385 dead and property losses reached $500 million (the equivalent of $8.7 billion today).

American industrialist, aviator and film producer Howard Hughes (1905 - 1976) climbs into the cockpit of his Northrop Gamma aircraft in preparation for breaking his own speed record for transcontinental U.S. flight at Burbank, California. He landed in Newark, New Jersey, 7 hours, 28 minutes and 25 seconds later, beating his 1936 record time by almost 2 hours and averaging 332 miles an hour for the 2,490 miles he travelled.

FEBRUARY

5	President Franklin D. Roosevelt proposes a plan to enlarge the Supreme Court of the United States.
11	A sit-down strike ends when General Motors recognizes the United Automobile Workers (UAW) union.

MARCH

The first issue of the comic book Detective Comics is published in the United States in March 1937. Twenty-seven issues later Detective Comics introduced Batman who would eventually become the star of the title. Because of its significance, issue #27 is widely considered one of the most valuable comic books in existence (with one copy selling for an incredible $1,075,500 in 2010). Detective Comics is the longest continually published comic magazine in American history.

2	The Steel Workers Organizing Committee, precursor to United Steelworkers, signs a collective bargaining agreement with U.S. Steel.
17	The Atherton Report (private investigator Edwin Atherton's report detailing vice and police corruption in San Francisco) is released.
18	In the worst school disaster in American history (in terms of lives lost) occurs at the New London School in New London, Texas. A catastrophic natural gas explosion kills in excess of 295 students and teachers.
18	The Mother Frances Hospital opens one day ahead of schedule in Tyler, Texas to care for victims of the New London School explosion.
25	It is revealed Quaker Oats is paying Babe Ruth $25,000 per year for ads.
26	William Henry Hastie becomes the first African-American appointed to a federal judgeship.
26	In Crystal City, Texas, spinach growers erect a statue of Popeye.

APRIL

| 12 | NLRB v. Jones & Laughlin Steel: The Supreme Court of the United States rules that the National Labor Relations Act is constitutional. |
| 17 | The animated short film Porky's Duck Hunt, directed by Tex Avery for the Looney Tunes series and featuring the debut of Daffy Duck, is released. |

MAY

	The U.S. goes into a recession which will last until June 1938 (there are over 7 million unemployed).
3	Margaret Mitchell wins the Pulitzer Prize for "Gone With the Wind".
6	The airship Hindenburg catches fire and is destroyed in New Jersey.
26	The Little Steel Strike starts with workers wanting better wages, benefits and working conditions. Within days 67,000 workers were off the job and it becomes one of the most violent strikes of the 1930s. Thousands of strikers were arrested, three hundred injured and eighteen died. The Little Steel companies eventually defeated the strike which lasted just over five months.
27	In California the Golden Gate Bridge opens to pedestrian traffic creating a vital link between San Francisco and Marin County. The next day President Franklin D. Roosevelt pushes a button in Washington, D.C. signalling the start of vehicle traffic over the Golden Gate Bridge.

The German passenger airship LZ 129 Hindenburg catches fire and is destroyed during its attempt to dock with its mooring mast at Naval Air Station Lakehurst in Manchester Township, New Jersey. Of the 97 people on board (36 passengers and 61 crewmen), there were 35 fatalities (13 passengers and 22 crewmen). One worker on the ground was also killed. The disaster was the subject of spectacular newsreel coverage which shattered public confidence in the giant passenger-carrying rigid airship and marked the abrupt end of the airship era.

JUNE

5	Henry Ford initiates 32 hour work week.
14	Pennsylvania becomes the first to celebrate Flag Day officially as a state holiday.
22	Joe Louis KOs James J Braddock to win the World Heavyweight Boxing Championship.

Joe Louis (197¼lbs) beat Jim Braddock (197lbs) by KO in round 8 of 15. Entering the fight against Louis, Braddock had only ever been knocked down twice and he had got up each time to win. Louis became the only person who managed to put him down for the referee's count of ten. Louis held the title for twelve years and defended it twenty-five times (both records for all weight divisions).

JULY

2	Amelia Earhart and navigator Fred Noonan disappear after taking off from New Guinea during Earhart's attempt to become the first woman to fly around the world.
2	A guard first stands post at the Tomb of the Unknowns in Washington, D.C. - continuous guard has been maintained there ever since.
4	The Lost Colony historical drama is first performed in an outdoor theatre in the location where it is set, Roanoke Island, North Carolina.
5	The canned precooked meat product Spam is introduced by the Hormel company.
22	New Deal: The United States Senate votes down President Franklin D. Roosevelt's proposal to add more justices to the Supreme Court of the United States.
24	Alabama drops rape charges against the so-called Scottsboro Boys.

AUGUST

5	Ranger (US) beats Endeavour II (England) in 17th America's Cup.
8	The Bonneville Dam on the Columbia River begins producing power.
18	W1XOJ becomes the first FM radio station after being granted a construction permit by the Federal Communications Commission (FCC).

SEPTEMBER

7	CBS broadcasts a two-and-a-half hour memorial concert nationwide on radio in memory of George Gershwin, live from the Hollywood Bowl. Many celebrities appear including Oscar Levant, Fred Astaire, Otto Klemperer, Lily Pons and members of the original cast of Porgy and Bess. The concert is recorded and released in full years later. The Los Angeles Philharmonic is the featured orchestra.
26	Street & Smith launches a half-hour radio program called The Shadow with Orson Welles in the title role.

OCTOBER

1	The Marijuana Tax Act becomes law in the United States.
1	U.S. Supreme Court associate justice Hugo Black, in a nationwide radio broadcast, refutes allegations of past involvement in the Ku Klux Klan.
5	Roosevelt gives his famous Quarantine Speech in Chicago.
15	Ernest Hemingway's novel To Have and Have Not is first published.

NOVEMBER

15	A U.S. congressional session takes place in air-conditioned chambers for the first time.
23	John Steinbeck's "Of Mice & Men" premieres at the Music Box Theatre on Broadway. Running for 207 performances, it starred Wallace Ford as George and Broderick Crawford as Lennie. The role of Crooks was performed by Leigh Whipper (the first African-American member of the Actors' Equity Association).

DECEMBER

12	Panay incident: Japanese bombers sink the American gunboat USS Panay. The Japanese claimed that they did not see the American flags painted on the deck of the gunboat, apologized and paid an indemnity.
12	Mae West makes a risqué guest appearance on the NBC Chase and Sanborn Hour that eventually results in her being banned from radio.
21	The first feature-length animated cartoon with sound, Walt Disney's Snow White and the Seven Dwarfs, opens and becomes a smash hit.
25	At the age of 70, legendary conductor Arturo Toscanini conducts the NBC Symphony Orchestra on radio for the first time. This first concert consists of music by Vivaldi, Mozart and Brahms. Millions tune in to listen including U.S. President Franklin D. Roosevelt.

UNDATED EVENTS FROM 1937

- Napoleon Hill's self-help book Think and Grow Rich is published. At the time of Hill's death in 1970, Think and Grow Rich had sold more than 20 million copies and by 2011 over 70 million copies had been sold worldwide.

U.S. PERSONALITIES

BORN IN 1937

Glen Albert Larson
January 3, 1937 -
November 14, 2014

Television producer and writer best known as the creator of the television series Alias Smith and Jones, Battlestar Galactica, Buck Rogers in the 25th Century, Quincy M.E., The Hardy Boys / Nancy Drew Mysteries, B.J. and the Bear, The Fall Guy, Magnum P.I. and Knight Rider. Larson has an Emmy Award, Grammy Award, two Edgar Awards and a star on the Hollywood Walk of Fame for his contributions to the television industry.

Dyan Cannon (born Samille Diane Friesen)
January 4, 1937

Film and television actress, director, screenwriter, editor and producer who has been nominated for three Academy Awards. Cannon made her film debut in 1960 in The Rise and Fall of Legs Diamond but her first major film role came in 1969's Bob & Carol & Ted & Alice, which earned her Academy Award and Golden Globe nominations. In 1978 she received another Oscar nomination and won a Golden Globe Award for Best Supporting Actress in Heaven Can Wait.

Roger S. Penske
February 20, 1937

Entrepreneur who has been extensively involved in professional racing for decades. Penske is most noted as the owner of the auto racing team Team Penske and has the most victories as an owner in the Indianapolis 500; 16 owner victories. A winning racer in the late 1950s, Penske was named 1961's Sports Car Club of America Driver of the Year by Sports Illustrated. As of September 2015 Penske has an estimated net worth of $1.95 billion.

Bob Lloyd Schieffer
February 25, 1937

Television journalist who is one of the few journalists to have covered all four of the major Washington national assignments: the White House, the Pentagon, United States Department of State and United States Congress. Schieffer was with CBS News from 1969 until his retirement in 2015, serving as the anchor on the Saturday edition of CBS Evening News for 23 years from 1973 to 1996 as well as the Chief Washington Correspondent from 1982 until 2015.

Jerry Reed Hubbard
March 20, 1937 -
September 1, 2008

A country music singer, guitarist, songwriter and actor who appeared in more than a dozen films and was known professionally as Jerry Reed. He won 3 Grammy Awards and was the Country Music Association Instrumentalist Of The Year in both 1970 and 1971. Some of his signature songs included "Guitar Man," "When You're Hot, You're Hot" and "East Bound and Down" (the theme song for the 1977 blockbuster Smokey and the Bandit in which Reed co-starred).

Henry Warren Beatty
March 30, 1937

Actor and filmmaker who has been nominated for fourteen Academy Awards winning Best Director for Reds (1981). Beatty is the first and only person to have been twice nominated for acting in, directing, writing and producing the same film; first with Heaven Can Wait (1978) and again with Reds. In 1999 he was awarded the Academy's highest honor, the Irving G. Thalberg Award. Beatty has also won six Golden Globe Awards.

Colin Luther Powell
April 5, 1937

Statesman and a retired four-star general in the United States Army. He was the 65th United States Secretary of State (serving under U.S. President George W. Bush from 2001 to 2005) becoming the first African American to serve in that position. During his military career Powell also served as National Security Advisor (1987-1989), as Commander of the U.S. Army Forces Command (1989) and as Chairman of the Joint Chiefs of Staff (1989-1993).

Merle Ronald Haggard
April 6, 1937 -
April 6, 2016

Singer, songwriter, guitarist, fiddler and instrumentalist. Along with Buck Owens, Haggard and his band the Strangers helped create the Bakersfield sound. He received many honors and awards for his music, including a Kennedy Center Honor (2010), a Grammy Lifetime Achievement Award (2006) and a BMI Icon Award (2006). He was also inducted into the Nashville Songwriters Hall of Fame (1977), the Country Music Hall of Fame (1994) and Oklahoma Music Hall of Fame (1997).

Robert Dean "Bobby" Hooks
April 18, 1937

Actor of films, television and stage, with a career as a producer and political activist to his credit. He is most recognizable to the public for his 100+ roles in films and television. Hooks has been regarded as a gifted artist who broke the color barriers in stage, film and television before the term "colorblind casting" even existed and a leading man when there were no African American matinee idols.

George Hosato Takei
April 20, 1937

Actor, director, author and activist. Takei is best known for his role as Hikaru Sulu, helmsman of the USS Enterprise in the television series Star Trek. He also portrayed the character in six Star Trek feature films and in an episode of Star Trek: Voyager. Takei's involvement in social media has brought him new fame and his Facebook page currently has over 9.8 million likes. He uses the page (started in 2011) to frequently share photos with original humorous commentary.

John Joseph "Jack" Nicholson
April 22, 1937

Actor and filmmaker whose 12 Academy Award nominations make him the most nominated male actor in the Academy's history. Nicholson has won the Academy Award for Best Actor twice for the drama One Flew Over the Cuckoo's Nest (1975) and for the romantic comedy As Good as It Gets (1997). He also won the Academy Award for Best Supporting Actor for the comedy-drama Terms of Endearment (1983) making him one of only three male actors to win three Academy Awards.

Sandra Dale "Sandy" Dennis
April 27, 1937 -
March 2, 1992

Theatre, television and film actress. Dennis made her television debut in 1956 in The Guiding Light and at the height of her career in the 1960s she won two Tony Awards as well as an Oscar for her performance in Who's Afraid of Virginia Woolf? (1966). Her last leading role was in The Indian Runner (1991) which also marked Sean Penn's debut as a film director. She died the following year from ovarian cancer.

Madeleine Jana Korbel Albright (born Marie Jana Korbelová)
May 15, 1937

Politician and diplomat who is the first woman to have become the United States Secretary of State. She was nominated by U.S. President Bill Clinton on December 5, 1996, and was unanimously confirmed by a U.S. Senate vote of 99-0. She was sworn in on January 23, 1997. In May 2012 she was awarded the Presidential Medal of Freedom by U.S. President Barack Obama. Albright is fluent in English, French, Russian and Czech; she also speaks and reads Polish and Serbo-Croatian.

Yvonne Joyce Craig
May 16, 1937 -
August 17, 2015

Ballet dancer and actress best known for her role as Batgirl in the 1960s television series Batman (the Huffington Post called her "a pioneer of female superheroes" for television). Craig starred in roles with Elvis Presley in two films: It Happened at the World's Fair (1963) and Kissin' Cousins (1964). She also starred in the 1966 cult sci-fi film Mars Needs Women and appeared in In Like Flint (1967) as a Russian ballet dancer opposite James Coburn.

Morgan Freeman
June 1, 1937

Actor and narrator who won an Academy Award in 2005 for Best Supporting Actor with Million Dollar Baby (2004). He has also received Oscar nominations for his performances in Street Smart (1987), Driving Miss Daisy (1989), The Shawshank Redemption (1994) and Invictus (2009). Morgan Freeman is ranked as the 3rd highest box office star of all time by IMDB with over $4.316 billion total box office gross (making an average of over $74 million per film).

David Bryant Mumford
June 11, 1937

Mathematician known for distinguished work in algebraic geometry and then for research into vision and pattern theory. Mumford was awarded a Fields Medal in 1974, was a MacArthur Fellow from 1987 to 1992 and won the Shaw Prize in 2006. In 2010 he was awarded the National Medal of Science. He is currently a University Professor Emeritus in the Division of Applied Mathematics at Brown University.

Waylon Arnold Jennings
June 15, 1937 -
February 13, 2002

Singer, songwriter, musician and actor. Jennings began playing guitar at eight and began performing at 12 on KVOW radio. His first band was The Texas Longhorns and in 1958 Buddy Holly arranged Jennings's first recording session. During his career Jennings also appeared in movies and television series. He was the balladeer for The Dukes of Hazzard, composing and singing the show's theme song. In 2001 he was inducted into the Country Music Hall of Fame.

John Davison "Jay" Rockefeller IV
June 18, 1937

United States Senator from West Virginia (1985-2015). He was first elected to the Senate in 1984, while in office as Governor of West Virginia, a position he held from 1977 to 1985. He became the state's senior senator when the long serving Sen. Robert Byrd died in June 2010. As a great-grandson of oil tycoon John D. Rockefeller he was the only serving politician of the prominent six-generation Rockefeller family. On January 11, 2013 Rockefeller announced that he would not seek re-election in 2014.

William Henry "Bill" Cosby, Jr.
July 12, 1937

Former stand-up comedian, actor, author and singer-songwriter. Cosby's start in stand-up comedy began at the "hungry i" in San Francisco and was followed by him landing a starring role in the 1960s television show I Spy. Using the Fat Albert character developed during his stand-up routines Cosby created the animated comedy TV series Fat Albert and the Cosby Kids (1972-1985). Cosby then produced and starred in The Cosby Show (1984-1992) which was rated as the No.1 show in America for five years (1984-1989).

Dustin Lee Hoffman
August 8, 1937

Actor and director with a career in film, television and theatre since 1960. Widely considered one of the finest actors in history, Hoffman first drew critical praise for starring in the play, Eh?. This achievement was soon followed by his breakthrough film role as Benjamin Braddock in The Graduate (1967). Hoffman won Academy Awards for Best Actor for Kramer vs. Kramer (1980) and Rain Man (1989), and has also won 6 Golden Globes, 4 BAFTAs, 3 Drama Desk Awards, a Genie Award and an Emmy.

Jacqueline Jill "Jackie" Collins, OBE
4 October 1937 -
19 September 2015

English born romance novelist who became a naturalized U.S citizen on May 6, 1960. After moving to Los Angeles in the 1960s she spent most of her career there. Collins wrote 32 novels all of which appeared on The New York Times bestsellers list. In total her books have sold over 500 million copies and have been translated into 40 languages, with eight of her novels also being adapted for the screen as either films or television miniseries. She was the younger sister of actress Joan Collins.

Loretta Jane Swit
November 4, 1937

Stage and television actress best known for her portrayal of Major Margaret "Hot Lips" Houlihan on M*A*S*H (1972-1983) for which she won two Emmy Awards. Swit was one of only four cast members to stay for all 11 seasons of the show. As well as guest-starring in many other shows such as Bonanza, The Love Boat, Win, Lose or Draw, Gunsmoke and The Muppet Show, in 1991 she won the Sarah Siddons Award for her work in Chicago theatre. Swit received a star on the Hollywood Walk of Fame in 1989.

James Gordon MacArthur
December 8, 1937 -
October 28, 2010

Actor who made his stage debut at Olney, Maryland in 1949 with a two-week stint in The Corn Is Green (his sister Mary was in the play and telephoned their mother to request that James go to Olney to be in it with her). He went on to have a long career starring in many roles on television and in film but is best known for the playing the part of Danny "Danno" Williams, the reliable second-in-command of the fictional Hawaiian State Police squad, in the long-running television series Hawaii Five-O.

Jane Fonda (born Jayne Seymour Fonda)
December 21, 1937

Actress, writer, political activist, former fashion model and fitness guru who made her Broadway debut in the 1960 play There Was a Little Girl. She rose to fame in 1960s films such as Period of Adjustment (1962), Sunday in New York (1963), Cat Ballou (1965), Barefoot in the Park (1967) and Barbarella (1968). She is a two-time Academy Award winner for Best Actress for her roles in the films Klute (1971) and Coming Home (1978). In 2014 was the recipient of the American Film Institute Life Achievement Award.

POPULAR MUSIC 1937

No.1	Benny Goodman	Sing, Sing, Sing
No.2	Count Basie	One O'Clock Jump
No.3	Bing Crosby	Sweet Leilani
No.4	Fred Astaire	They Can't Take That Away From Me
No.5	Duke Ellington	Caravan
No.6	Shep Fields	That Old Feeling
No.7	Tommy Dorsey	Marie
No.8	George Formby	Leaning On A Lamp-Post
No.9	Ella Fitzgerald	Goodnight, My Love
No.10	Guy Lombardo	September In The Rain

Benny Goodman
Sing, Sing, Sing (With A Swing)

Label:	Written by:	Length:
Victor	Louis Prima	8 mins 43 secs

Benjamin David 'Benny' Goodman (May 30, 1909 - June 13, 1986) was a jazz and swing musician, clarinettist and bandleader known as the 'King of Swing'. The song Sing, Sing, Sing was arranged by Jimmy Mundy and unlike most big band arrangements of that era which were limited to three minutes (so that they could be recorded on one side of a standard 10-inch 78-rpm record), this version was an extended work lasting 8 min 43 secs and took up both sides of a 12-inch 78.

Count Basie
One O'Clock Jump

Label:	Written by:	Length:
Decca	Count Basie	3 mins 2 secs

William James "Count" Basie (August 21, 1904 - April 26, 1984) was a jazz pianist, organist, bandleader, and composer. "One O'Clock Jump" became the theme song of the Count Basie Orchestra and they used it to close each of their concerts for the next half century.

Bing Crosby
Sweet Leilani

Label:	Written by:	Length:
Decca	Harry Owens	3 mins 7 secs

Harry Lillis 'Bing' Crosby, Jr. (May 3, 1903 - October 14, 1977) was an actor and singer whose trademark warm bass-baritone voice made him the best-selling recording artist of the 20th century. "Sweet Leilani" was featured in the film Waikiki Wedding (1937) and won an Academy Award for Best Original Song.

Fred Astaire
They Can't Take That Away From Me

Label:	Written by:	Length:
Brunswick	George & Ira Gershwin	3 mins 38 secs

Fred Astaire (May 10, 1899 - June 22, 1987) was a dancer, choreographer, singer, musician and actor. His stage and subsequent film and television careers spanned a total of 76 years. "They Can't Take That Away From Me" featured in the film Shall We Dance (1937).

⑤ Duke Ellington
Caravan

Label:	Written by:	Length:
Brunswick	Ellington / Tizol	2 mins 47 secs

Edward Kennedy "Duke" Ellington (April 29, 1899 - May 24, 1974) was a composer, pianist, and bandleader of a jazz orchestra which he led from 1923 until his death. In a career spanning over fifty years Ellington wrote more than one thousand compositions and his extensive body of work is the largest personal jazz legacy to ever be recorded.

⑥ Shep Fields & His Rippling Rhythm Orchestra
That Old Feeling

Label:	Written by:	Length:
Bluebird Records	Sammy Fain / Lew Brown	2 mins 28 secs

Shep Fields (September 12, 1910 - February 23, 1981) was born Saul Feldman in Brooklyn, New York and was the band leader for his Rippling Rhythm Orchestra during the Big Band era of the 1930s. In 1937 "That Old Feeling" was an immediate hit and was featured in the film Vogues of 1938 (1937).

7 Tommy Dorsey
Marie

Label:	Written by:	Length:
RCA Victor	Irving Berlin	3 mins 16 secs

Thomas Francis "Tommy" Dorsey, Jr. (November 19, 1905 - November 26, 1956) was a jazz trombonist, composer, conductor and bandleader of the Big Band era. He was known as the "Sentimental Gentleman of Swing" because of his smooth-toned trombone playing. He is best remembered for standards such as "Opus One", "Song of India", "Marie", "On Treasure Island", and his biggest hit single "I'll Never Smile Again".

8 George Formby
Leaning On A Lamp-Post

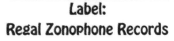

Label:	Written by:	Length:
Regal Zonophone Records	Noel Gay	3 mins 1 sec

George Hoy Booth Formby, OBE (May 26, 1904 - March 6, 1961) was an actor, singer-songwriter and comedian who became known to a worldwide audience through his films of the 1930s and 1940s. On stage, screen and record, he sang light comical songs, usually playing the ukulele or banjolele, and became the UK's highest-paid entertainer.

⑨ Ella Fitzgerald
Goodnight, My Love

Label:	Written by:	Length:
Victor	Harry Revel / Mack Gordon	3 mins 8 secs

Ella Jane Fitzgerald (April 25, 1917 - June 15, 1996) was a jazz singer often referred to as the First Lady of Song, the Queen of Jazz and Lady Ella. This Goodman recording of "Goodnight, My Love" has an unbilled vocal by Ella Fitzgerald because at the time she was the band vocalist for Decca recording artist Chick Webb. Following Victor's release of this and two other Goodman-Fitzgerald sides, Decca threatened legal action and the 78s were withdrawn from sale.

⑩ Guy Lombardo
September In The Rain

Label:	Written by:	Length:
Victor	Harry Warren / Al Dubin	2 mins 58 secs

Gaetano Alberto 'Guy' Lombardo (June 19, 1902 - November 5, 1977) was a bandleader and violinist of Italian descent. Forming The Royal Canadians in 1924 with his brothers Carmen, Lebert and Victor, Lombardo led the group to international success. The Lombardo's are believed to have sold between 100 and 300 million records during their lifetimes.

TOP FILMS 1937

1. Snow White And The Seven Dwarfs
2. The Good Earth
3. One Hundred Men And A Girl
4. Topper
5. Wee Willie Winkie

OSCARS

Best Film: The Life of Emile Zola

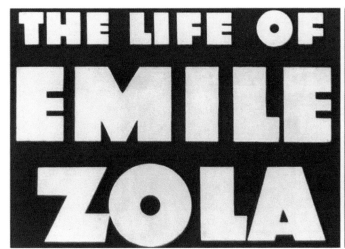

Best Director: Leo McCarey
(The Awful Truth)
Best Actor: Spencer Tracy
(Captains Courageous)
Best Actress: Luise Rainer
(The Good Earth)
Best Supporting Actor: Joseph Schildkraut
(The Life of Emile Zola)
Best Supporting Actress: Alice Brady
(In Old Chicago)

SNOW WHITE AND THE SEVEN DWARFS

Directed by: 6 Credited Directors - Runtime: 83 minutes

HIS FIRST FULL LENGTH FEATURE PRODUCTION

Walt Disney's

Snow White
and the Seven Dwarfs
in the Marvelous
MULTIPLANE TECHNICOLOR

© W D P

Distributed by RKO Radio Pictures, Inc.

Snow White takes refuge in a house inhabited by seven dwarfs to hide from her stepmother, the wicked Queen.

1937 Gross: $21,800,000 / Total Gross: $184,925,485

STARRING

Adriana Caselotti
Born: May 16, 1916
Died: January 19, 1997

Character:
Snow White (uncredited)

Voice actress and singer, born in Bridgeport, Connecticut. In 1935, after a brief stint as a chorus girl at MGM, Walt Disney hired Caselotti as the voice of his heroine Snow White paying her a total of $970 for working on the film. Under contract to Disney he then prevented her from appearing in further films and other media to stop her voice being used elsewhere (so not to spoil the illusion of Snow White).

Harry Stockwell
Born: April 27, 1902
Died: July 19, 1984

Character:
Prince (uncredited)

Actor and singer who was born in Kansas City, Missouri. Stockwell made his film debut in Strike Up the Band (1935) but his claim to fame was providing the voice of "The Prince" in this Walt Disney animated classic. Stockwell was also a noted Broadway performer and in 1943, he succeeded Alfred Drake as "Curly" in the lead role in Oklahoma!

Lucille La Verne
Born: November 7, 1872
Died: March 4, 1945

Character:
Queen/Witch (uncredited)

Actress known for her appearances in early color films as well as for her triumphs on the American stage. She made her Broadway debut in 1888 and became a leading lady with some of the best stock companies in America. Her biggest stage triumph came in 1923 with over 3,000 performances in the hit play Sun Up. Her best-known movie part is that of the voice of the Evil Queen/Old Hag in Snow White And The Seven Dwarfs.

TRIVIA

Goofs

When Snow White first enters the dwarfs' house the animals follow her in. Near the door there are two rabbits. As one of the rabbits passes behind the other it changes into a brown squirrel.

When Snow White is kissing all the dwarfs' foreheads and she goes to kiss Dopey you hear her say "Oh, Dopey!" but her lips never move.

At the end of "The Silly Song" there's a cutaway to Dopey playing the drums but at the same time he also appears standing atop of Sneezy.

When Doc is assaying the (already cut) gemstones from the mine, he puts the jeweller's loupe into his eye backwards.

Doc's lantern disappears when he and the other dwarfs reach the house after their work in the mine.

Interesting Facts   The films had 6 directors; David Hand the supervising director and William Cottrell, Wilfred Jackson, Larry Morey, Perce Pearce and Ben Sharpsteen who were the sequence directors.

At a recording session, Lucille La Verne, the voice of the Wicked Queen, was told by Walt Disney's animators that they needed an older, raspier version of the Queen's voice for the Old Witch. Ms. Laverne stepped out of the recording booth, returned a few minutes later, and gave a perfect "Old Hag's voice" that stunned the animators. When asked how she did it, she replied, "Oh, I just took my teeth out."

This was the first ever full-length animated feature film to come out of the U.S. (The world's first ever animated feature films were El apóstol (1917) and Sin dejar rastros (1918) by Quirino Cristiani but both films are considered lost).

It's widely known that every country where the movie has been translated has its own set of seven names for the Dwarfs, including Germany, home of the original fairy tale. However, in the original tale (by brothers Jacob Grimm & Wilhelm Grimm) the dwarfs have no individual names at all.

The film's initial budget was $250,000 but as it transpired the final budget was actually in excess of $1.4 million - a huge amount for any film at the time.

25 songs were written for the movie but only eight were used.

In 1994 Adriana Caselotti (who voiced Snow White) was named a Disney Legend making her the first woman to receive the award in the voice category.

Quotes   **Snow White:** Supper's not quite ready. You'll just have time to wash.
Dwarfs: (in unison) Wash?
Grumpy: (scoffs) I knew there's a catch to it!

THE GOOD EARTH

Directed by: Sidney Franklin - Runtime: 138 minutes

Wang, a poor Chinese farmer, marries freed slave O-Lan and starts raising a family. The story follows their rise to prosperity through hard times, famine and revolution.

STARRING

Paul Muni
Born: September 22, 1895
Died: August 25, 1967

Character:
Wang Lung

Stage and film actor who started his acting career in the Yiddish theatre. During the 1930s he was considered one of the most prestigious actors at Warner Brothers studios. He made 25 films in total and won the Academy Award for Best Actor for his role in The Story of Louis Pasteur (1936). He also starred in numerous Broadway plays and won the Tony Award for Best Actor in a Play for Inherit the Wind (1955).

Luise Rainer
Born: January 12, 1910
Died: December 30, 2014

Character:
O-Lan

Film actress who was the first actor to win multiple Academy Awards winning Best Actress in The Great Ziegfeld (1936) and The Good Earth. Rainer began acting in Germany at age 16 and after years of acting on stage and in films in Austria and Germany she was discovered by MGM talent scouts who signed her to a 3 year contract in 1935. Rainer made her final appearance for MGM in 1938 when she then decided to leave the film industry.

Walter Connolly
Born: April 8, 1887
Died: May 28, 1940

Character:
Uncle

Character actor who appeared in almost fifty films between 1914 and 1939 and twenty-two Broadway productions between 1916 and 1935. His best known film is It Happened One Night (1934) with Clark Gable and Claudette Colbert where Connolly played the part of millionaire Alexander Andrews. The film became the first movie to win all five major Academy Awards (Best Picture, Director, Actor, Actress and Screenplay).

TRIVIA

Goofs

When Wang Lung and his family are waiting for the train the locomotive that passes behind them has a number clearly visible on the front of the boiler. When the same train is seen approaching the crowds the locomotive does not have a number and is of a different design.

During the drought some black vultures are seen on a roof. These are native American birds not seen in the wild in China.

Interesting Facts

Chinese-born Anna May Wong desperately wanted the role of O-Lan. She tested for the role but producer Irving Thalberg had already cast Paul Muni in the lead role and was unable to cast Wong as Muni's wife. The Hays Code prohibited actors of different races from playing husband/wife on film to avoid offending white audiences in the segregated American South. Thalberg offered her the role of Lotus instead but a distraught Anna May Wong turned it down.

CONTINUED

Interesting Facts   Because of the general political instability at the time and wars throughout China with the Nationalist government fighting off a Japanese invasion while at the same time battling Communist rebels and various powerful local warlords this naturally precluded shooting location footage there. MGM therefore decided to turn a 500-acre farm in Chatsworth, CA, into Chinese farmland and shot the "location" footage there instead.

Special effects experts were unable to produce an authentic looking locust plague. Just as they were about to abandon the scene they received word that there was a real locust plague taking place several states away and a camera crew was dispatched immediately to capture it on film.

When Irving Thalberg negotiated with Warner Brothers to cast Paul Muni, Muni declared, "I'm about as Chinese as Herbert Hoover." He was cast in the role but Thalberg had to lend Clark Gable and Leslie Howard to Warner Brothers to secure Muni's services.

Producer Irving Thalberg died 4½ months before the film's Los Angeles premiere. The movie was dedicated to him "as his last great achievement."

One Hundred Men and a Girl

Directed by: Henry Koster - Runtime: 84 minutes

The daughter of a struggling musician forms a symphony orchestra made up of his unemployed friends and through persistence, charm and a few misunderstandings, is able to get Leopold Stokowski to lead them in a concert that leads to a radio contract.

STARRING

Deanna Durbin
Born: December 4, 1921
Died: April 20, 2013

Character:
Patricia Cardwell

Actress and singer, who appeared in musical films in the 1930s and 1940s. Durbin made her first film appearance with Judy Garland in Every Sunday (1936) and subsequently signed a contract with Universal Studios. Her success as the ideal teenaged daughter in films such as Three Smart Girls (1936) was credited with saving the studio from bankruptcy. In 1938, at the age of 17, Durbin was awarded the Academy Juvenile Award.

Leopold Stokowski
Born: April 18, 1882
Died: September 13, 1977

Character:
Leopold Stokowski

British conductor of Polish and Irish descent. One of the leading conductors of the early and mid-20th Century, he is best known for his long association with the Philadelphia Orchestra and for appearing in the film Fantasia. He was especially noted for his free-hand conducting style that spurned the traditional baton and for obtaining a characteristically sumptuous sound from the orchestras he directed.

Adolphe Menjou
Born: February 18, 1890
Died: October 29, 1963

Character:
John Cardwell

Actor whose career spanned both silent films and talkies. His most popular films include The Sheik (1921) with Rudolph Valentino, Charles Chaplin's A Woman of Paris (1923), Morocco (1930) with Marlene Dietrich and Gary Cooper, A Star Is Born (1937) with Janet Gaynor and Fredric March, and Stanley Kubrick's Paths Of Glory (1957) with Kirk Douglas. He was nominated for an Academy Award for The Front Page (1931).

TRIVIA

Interesting Facts   Leopold Stokowski recorded the classical music in the film at the Philadelphia Academy of Music using the Philadelphia Orchestra (of which he was still principal guest conductor). It was done on a multi-channel sound system, the first time one was ever used to record music in a film. The musicians seen in the film however were Los Angeles based players doing what was called "sideline" (seen but not heard, merely miming to a prerecorded soundtrack played by others).

On July 23, 1949 this film double-billed with The Mikado (1939) being revived at the Little Carnegie Theatre in Manhattan. On August 31, 1949, Universal (by then called Universal International) concluded its 13-year association with Deanna Durbin.

Deanna Durbin's vocal coach was Spanish operatic bass Andrés de Segurola.

Quotes

Leopold Stokowski: *[Patsy has come to apologize for telling a newspaper that Stokowski would be conducting her orchestra of jobless musicians]* But why did you do it? You must have had a reason.

Patricia "Patsy" Cardwell: Oh, yes! I had a hundred reasons! Would you like to hear them?

Leopold Stokowski: I certainly would.

Patricia "Patsy" Cardwell: *[Goes to the door of his study and counts]* One! Two! Three! Four!

[Stokowski suddenly hears "Hungarian Rhapsody" and they both go out onto his balcony overlooking the entryway. The 100 men are standing on the stairway, playing]

Patricia "Patsy" Cardwell: Those are my reasons. I thought you'd like to hear them.

Topper

Directed by: Norman Z. McLeod - Runtime: 97 minutes

A fun-loving couple (finding that they have died and are now ghosts) decide to shake up the stuffy lifestyle of their friend bank president Cosmo Topper.

STARRING

Cary Grant
Born: January 18, 1904
Died: November 29, 1986

Character:
George Kerby

British-American actor known as one of classic Hollywood's definitive leading men. He began a career in Hollywood in the early 1930s and became known for his transatlantic accent, light-hearted approach to acting, comic timing and debonair demeanor. He was twice nominated for the Academy Award for Best Actor for his roles in Penny Serenade (1941) and None but the Lonely Heart (1944).

Constance Bennett
Born: October 22, 1904
Died: July 24, 1965

Character:
Marion Kerby

Film actress and a major Hollywood star during the 1920s and 1930s. During the early 1930s she was for a time the highest-paid actress in Hollywood and one of the most popular. She is best known today for her leading roles in What Price Hollywood? (1932), Topper and its sequel Topper Takes a Trip (1938). Bennett also had a prominent supporting role in Greta Garbo's last film Two-Faced Woman (1941).

Roland Young
Born: November 11, 1887
Died: June 5, 1953

Character:
Cosmo Topper

Actor who made his first stage appearance in London's West End in Find The Woman in 1908. Young made his film debut in the silent film Sherlock Holmes (1922) in which he played Watson opposite John Barrymore as Holmes. He achieved one of the most important successes of his career in Topper for which he received a nomination for the Academy Award for Best Supporting Actor.

TRIVIA

Goofs

When George and Marion walk into the club and are sitting down someone seated at the table calls George "Cary".

You can see through various people and objects when George and Marion appear and disappear.

Interesting Facts

The commercial and critical success of this film led director Norman Z. McLeod to include much of the principal cast in his next film, Merrily We Live (1938). Constance Bennett, Alan Mowbray and Billie Burke all received major parts in McLeod's next work, with Mowbray reprising his role as a stuffy butler and with Burke again playing the matriarchal head of a household.

This was the first black & white film to be "colorized" in 1985.

CONTINUED

Interesting Facts   Hal Roach immediately wanted Cary Grant to play George Kerby but he had difficulty getting the actor to agree to play the part because Grant was concerned about the supernatural aspects of the story. Assurance from Roach that the screwball aspects of the story would be played up, plus a fee of $50,000, were sufficient to convince Grant to do the film.

This was the second ever film appearance of Lana Turner (she was uncredited and had no lines).

Songwriter and pianist Hoagy Carmichael makes an uncredited cameo appearance early in the film as the piano player in the sequence where George and Marion are on the town the night before the meeting at the bank. He introduces the song "Old Man Moon" which is sung by George and Marion. This was Carmichael's screen debut. As the couple leave the bar, George says "(Good) night" and Carmichael replies "So long, see ya next time."

Quotes   *[George and Marion watch a drunk Topper laying on the floor passed out]*
Marion Kerby: I don't think he's ever had a drink in his life.
George Kerby: Poor Topper.
Marion Kerby: Poor Topper.
Cosmo Topper: *[mutters]* Poor Topper.
George Kerby: You keep out of this.

Hotel Manager: Perhaps you can explain the red on this cigarette.
Cosmo Topper: Yes, I... cut my tongue when I was shaving this morning.

 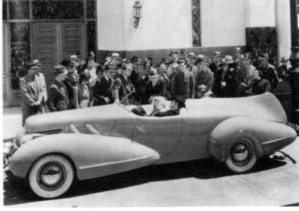

WEE WILLIE WINKIE

Directed by: John Ford - Runtime: 100 minutes

A story about the British presence in nineteenth century India when a young girl travels with her mother to join her paternal grandfather at the post he commands.

STARRING

Shirley Temple
Born: April 23, 1928
Died: February 10, 2014

Character:
Priscilla Williams

American film and television actress, singer, dancer and public servant. Temple began her film career in 1932 at the age of three and was Hollywood's number one box-office star from 1935 through 1938. As an adult she entered politics and became a diplomat serving as US Ambassador to Ghana and later to Czechoslovakia. She also served as Chief of Protocol of the United States.

Victor McLaglen
Born: December 10, 1886
Died: November 7, 1959

Character:
Sergeant MacDuff

An English boxer and WW1 veteran who became a successful film actor in the 1920s when he moved to Hollywood. He became a popular character actor with a particular knack for playing drunks. He also usually played Irishmen leading many film fans to assume he was Irish rather than English. McLaglen won the Academy Award for Best Actor for his role in The Informer (1935).

Sir Charles Aubrey Smith, CBE
Born: July 21, 1863
Died: December 20, 1948

Character:
Colonel Williams

An England Test cricketer who became a stage and film actor. Known to film-goers as C. Aubrey Smith he starred alongside many screen legends such as Greta Garbo, Elizabeth Taylor, Vivien Leigh, Clark Gable, Laurence Olivier, Ronald Colman, Maurice Chevalier and Gary Cooper. His bushy eyebrows, beady eyes, handlebar moustache and height of 6'4" made him one of the most recognisable faces in Hollywood.

TRIVIA

Interesting Facts

Shirley Temple disclosed in her autobiography that this was the only film she made in which she received an onscreen spanking, much to the chagrin of June Lang who played the spanker and feared that her career would suffer as a result of the audience seeing the popular Shirley being treated in this fashion. The scene was shot but was eventually cut from the film.

The original story by Rudyard Kipling was about a boy, Percival Williams, but this was changed to a girl, Priscilla Williams, in order for Shirley Temple to play the role.

Production of Wee Willie Winkie had to be moved from the Fox studio lot to Chatsworth, California, owing to intense conflicts taking place between labor unions and Hollywood studios. During one standoff a Fox studio messenger visiting the set nearly had a light dropped on his head after scolding a stagehand who complained about working conditions.

CONTINUED

Interesting Facts   On March 29, 1938, 20th Century Fox was awarded £3,500 in a trial for civil libel brought against British novelist Graham Greene who was judged to have written a defamatory review of Wee Willie Winkie for the magazine Night and Day. Greene's review which had said that the nine-year-old Shirley Temple displayed "a dubious coquetry" which appealed to "middle-aged men and clergymen" resulted in the magazine folding.

Quotes   **Sgt. Donald MacDuff:** You made a very good beginning.
Priscilla Williams: Yes, but whoever head of a solider named Priscilla?
Sgt. Donald MacDuff: Aye, that's the point. You couldn't take Private Pricilla very seriously, could you? We'll have to find a new name for you.
[pauses]
Sgt. Donald MacDuff: I got it! I got it! Wee Willie Winkie.
Priscilla Williams: Wee Willie Winkie?
[They both laugh]
Priscilla Williams: Was he a friend of yours?
Sgt. Donald MacDuff: Nah, he was a lad in an old scotch rhyme. Wee Willie Winkie ran through the town... Wee Willie Winkie ran through the town... he ran through the... well, he was a lad who was always getting himself into difficulties.

SPORTING WINNERS

DON BUDGE - TENNIS

ASSOCIATED PRESS - MALE ATHLETE OF THE YEAR

John Donald "Don" Budge
Born: June 13, 1915 in Oakland, California
Died: January 26, 2000 in Scranton, Pennsylvania
Singles Tennis Highest Ranking: No.1

Don Budge was an American tennis champion who was a World No.1 player first as an amateur and then as a professional. He is most famous as the first ever player (and only American male) to win all four Grand Slam tournaments in the same year. He was also only the second male player to win all four Grand Slams after Fred Perry and is still the youngest to achieve that feat. In total Budge won a total of 14 Grand Slam tournaments (including a record 6 consecutive Grand Slam singles titles) and 4 Pro Slams, the latter achieved on three different surfaces. Budge was considered to have one of the best backhands in the history of tennis.

Grand Slam Titles:

	Singles	Doubles	Mixed Doubles
Australian Open	1938	-	-
French Open	1938	-	-
Wimbledon	1937 / 1938	1937 / 1938	1937 / 1938
U.S. Open	1937 / 1938	1936 / 1938	1937 / 1938

In 1942 Budge joined the United States Army Air Force to serve in World War II. After the war Budge played for a few years recording his last significant victory in 1954 in a North American tour beating Pancho Gonzales (by then the best player in the world). After retiring from competition Budge coached and conducted tennis clinics for children and was inducted into the International Tennis Hall of Fame at Newport, Rhode Island in 1964.

KATHERINE RAWLS - SWIMMING
ASSOCIATED PRESS - FEMALE ATHLETE OF THE YEAR

Photo 2: 3m Springboard Berlin Olympic medallists (L-R) Poynton-Hill, Gestring and Rawls.

Katherine Louise Rawls
Born: June 14, 1917 in Nashville, Tennessee
Died: April 8, 1982 in White Sulphur Springs, West Virginia

Katherine Louise Rawls, also known by her married names Katherine Thompson and Katherine Green, was an American competition swimmer and diver. She was the United States national champion in multiple events during the 1930s winning a total of 33 U.S. national titles: 5 in diving and 28 in swimming (both indoors at the Spring Nationals and outdoors at the Summer Nationals).

Olympic Games:

Olympics	Event	Medal
1932 Los Angeles	3m Springboard	Silver
1936 Berlin	3m Springboard	Silver
1936 Berlin	4x100m Freestyle	Bronze

In 1937, hours after disembarking at San Francisco after a swimming tour of Japan, she commenced a three-day streak at the Nationals which produced an unprecedented four individual swimming titles. For this she was named Associated Press Female Athlete of the Year for 1937 and polled third for the James E. Sullivan Award. In 1938 she retained all four National titles. At the time she was holder of 18 national swimming records in breaststroke, freestyle, and medley events and had been undefeated in medley races for eight years.

Rawls retired from swimming when the 1940 Olympics were cancelled owing to the outbreak of World War II. She became one of the initial 28 pilots who formed the Women's Auxiliary Ferrying Squadron in 1942, stationed at Detroit, transporting military cargo by air as part of the U.S. war effort. After the war Rawls was a swimming instructor for 20 years at the Greenbrier Hotel in White Sulphur Springs, West Virginia and in 1965 she was one of the inaugural inductees to the International Swimming Hall of Fame.

GOLF

THE MASTERS - BYRON NELSON

The Masters Tournament is the first of the majors to be played each year and unlike the other major championships it is played at the same location - Augusta National Golf Club, Georgia. This was the 4th Masters Tournament and was held April 1-4 with 25 year old Byron Nelson winning the first of his five major titles. The total prize fund was $5,000 with Nelson taking home $1,500.

U.S. OPEN - RALPH GULDAHL

The U.S. Open Championship (established in 1895) was held June 10-12 at the South Course of Oakland Hills Country Club in Birmingham, Michigan, a suburb northwest of Detroit. Ralph Guldahl won $1,000 and the first of his two consecutive U.S. Opens by two strokes to runner-up Sam Snead who was making his U.S. Open debut. Guldahl won the title with 19 clubs in his bag as the USGA rule (4-4) regarding a maximum of 14 clubs only went into effect the following January.

PGA CHAMPIONSHIP - DENNY SHUTE

The 1937 and 20th PGA Championship was played May 24-30 at Pittsburgh Field Club in Fox Chapel, Pennsylvania, a suburb northeast of Pittsburgh. Then a match play championship, Denny Shute won his second consecutive PGA Championship in less than seven months, defeating Harold "Jug" McSpaden in 37 holes (the previous edition in 1936 was held in November at Pinehurst, North Carolina). The total prize fund was $9,200 and the winner's share was $1,000.

Byron Nelson

Ralph Guldahl

Denny Shute

WORLD SERIES - NEW YORK YANKEES

New York Yankees   4 - 1   **New York Giants**

Total attendance: 238,142 - Average attendance: 47,628
Winning player's share: $6,471 - Losing player's share: $4,490

The World Series is the annual championship series of Major League Baseball, played since 1903 between the American League (AL) champion team and the National League (NL) champion and is determined through a best-of-seven playoff.

The 1937 World Series featured the defending champions the New York Yankees and the New York Giants in a rematch of the 1936 Series. The Yankees won in five games for their second championship in a row and their sixth in fifteen years. The Series was the first in which a team (in this case the Yankees) did not commit a single error. Game 4 ended with the final World Series innings ever pitched by Hall of Famer Carl Hubbell who during the ninth inning gave up Hall of Famer Lou Gehrig's final Series home run.

	Date	Score	Location	Time	Att.
1	Oct 6	New York Giants - 1 **New York Yankees - 8**	Yankee Stadium	2:20	60,573
2	Oct 7	New York Giants - 1 **New York Yankees - 8**	Yankee Stadium	2:11	57,675
3	Oct 8	**New York Yankees - 5** New York Giants - 1	Polo Grounds	2:07	37,385
4	Oct 9	New York Yankees - 3 **New York Giants - 7**	Polo Grounds	1:57	44,293
5	Oct 10	**New York Yankees - 4** New York Giants - 2	Polo Grounds	2:06	38,216

HORSE RACING

War Admiral, the fourth Triple Crown winner following Sir Barton, Gallant Fox and Omaha.

War Admiral (May 2, 1934 - October 30, 1959) was an American thoroughbred racehorse best known as the fourth winner of the American Triple Crown and Horse of the Year in 1937. War Admiral was foaled at Faraway Farm in Lexington and was the offspring of Man o' War who was widely regarded as the greatest American racehorse of his time. During his career, toward the end of the Great Depression, War Admiral won 21 of his 26 starts with earnings of $273,240.

KENTUCKY DERBY - WAR ADMIRAL

The Kentucky Derby is held annually at Churchill Downs in Louisville, Kentucky on the first Saturday in May. The race is a Grade I stakes race for three-year-olds and is one and a quarter miles in length.

PREAKNESS STAKES - WAR ADMIRAL

The Preakness Stakes is held on the third Saturday in May each year at Pimlico Race Course in Baltimore, Maryland. It is a Grade I race run over a distance of 9.5 furlongs (1 3/16 miles) on dirt.

BELMONT STAKES - WAR ADMIRAL

The Belmont Stakes is Grade I race held every June at Belmont Park in Elmont, New York. It is 1.5 miles in length and open to three-year-old thoroughbreds. It takes place on a Saturday between June 5 and June 11.

FOOTBALL - NFL CHAMPIONSHIP

CHAMPIONSHIP GAME

Washington Redskins   28 - 21   **Chicago Bears**

Played: December 12, 1937 at Wrigley Field in Chicago.
Attendance: 15,878

The 1937 NFL season was the 18th regular season of the National Football League. The Cleveland Rams joined the league as an expansion team meanwhile the Redskins relocated from Boston, Massachusetts to Washington, D.C. The season ended when the Washington Redskins defeated the Chicago Bears in the NFL Championship Game.

Conference Results:

Eastern Conference

Team	P	W	L	T	PCT	PF	PA
Washington Redskins	**11**	**8**	**3**	**0**	**.727**	**195**	**120**
New York Giants	11	6	3	2	.667	128	109
Pittsburgh Pirates	11	4	7	0	.364	122	145
Brooklyn Dodgers	11	3	7	1	.300	82	174
Philadelphia Eagles	11	2	8	1	.200	86	177

Western Conference

Team	P	W	L	T	PCT	PF	PA
Chicago Bears	**11**	**9**	**1**	**1**	**.900**	**201**	**100**
Green Bay Packers	11	7	4	0	.636	220	122
Detroit Lions	11	7	4	0	.636	180	105
Chicago Cardinals	11	5	5	1	.500	135	165
Cleveland Rams	11	1	10	0	.091	75	207

P= Games Played, W = Wins, L = Losses, T = Ties,
PCT= Winning Percentage, PF= Points For, PA = Points Against

League Leaders

Statistic	Name	Team	Yards
Passing	Sammy Baugh	Washington Redskins	1127
Rushing	Cliff Battles	Washington Redskins	874
Receiving	Gaynell Tinsley	Chicago Cardinals	675

HOCKEY: 1936-37 NHL SEASON

The 1936-37 NHL season was the 20th season of the National Hockey League. Eight teams each played 48 games. The Detroit Red Wings were the Stanley Cup winners as they beat the New York Rangers three games to two in the final series.

Final Standings:

	American Division	GP	W	L	T	GF	GA	Pts
1	**Detroit Red Wings**	48	25	14	9	128	102	59
2	Boston Bruins	48	23	18	7	120	110	53
3	New York Rangers	48	19	20	9	117	106	47
4	Chicago Black Hawks	48	14	27	7	99	131	35

	Canadian Division	GP	W	L	T	GF	GA	Pts
1	**Montreal Canadiens**	48	24	18	6	115	111	54
2	Montreal Maroons	48	22	17	9	126	110	53
3	Toronto Maple Leafs	48	22	21	5	119	115	49
4	New York Americans	48	15	29	4	122	161	34

Scoring Leaders:

	Player	Team	Goals	Assists	Points
1	**Sweeney Schriner**	**New York Americans**	21	25	46
2	Syl Apps	Toronto Maple Leafs	16	29	45
3	Marty Barry	Detroit Red Wings	17	27	44

Hart Trophy (Most Valuable Player): Babe Siebert - Montreal Canadiens
Vezina Trophy (Fewest Goals Allowed): Normie Smith - Detroit Red Wings

STANLEY CUP

Detroit Red Wings

3 - 2

New York Rangers

Series Summary:

	Date	Home Team	Result	Road Team
1	April 6	Detroit Red Wings	1-5	**New York Rangers**
2	April 8	New York Rangers	2-4	**Detroit Red Wings**
3	April 11	**New York Rangers**	1-0	Detroit Red Wings
4	April 13	New York Rangers	0-1	**Detroit Red Wings**
5	April 15	New York Rangers	0-3	**Detroit Red Wings**

INDIANAPOLIS 500 - WILBUR SHAW

The 25th International 500-Mile Sweepstakes was held at the Indianapolis Motor Speedway on Monday May 31, 1937. With temperatures topping out at 92°F it is one of the hottest days on record for the Indy 500. Late in the race Wilbur Shaw held a comfortable lead and had lapped second place Ralph Hepburn. With about 20 laps to go however Shaw's car had been leaking oil and had nearly lost all of the oil out of the crankcase. In addition the right rear tire was heavily worn. Shaw slowed down considerably in an effort to nurse his car to the finish line. As the laps dwindled down Ralph Hepburn was closing dramatically. Shaw was largely defenseless as he was carefully nursing the car around. On the final lap Hepburn pulled to within a few seconds and by the last turn he was directly behind Shaw and looking to pass him for the win. With nothing to lose Shaw floored the accelerator and pulled away down the final straight. He held off Hepburn for the win (by 2.16 seconds) making it the closest finish in Indy 500 history to that point. The margin would stand as the closest finish ever at Indy until 1982.

BOSTON MARATHON

WALTER YOUNG

The Boston Marathon is the oldest annual marathon in the world and dates back to 1897.

Race result:

1. **Walter Young (CAN)**   **2:33:20**
2. John A. Kelley (USA)   2:39:02
3. Leslie Pawson (USA)   2:41:46

TENNIS - U.S. NATIONAL CHAMPIONSHIPS

Mens Singles Champion - Don Budge - United States
Ladies Singles Champion - Anita Lizana - Chile

The 1937 U.S. National Championships (now known as the U.S. Open) took place on the outdoor grass courts at the West Side Tennis Club, Forest Hills in New York. The tournament ran from September 2-11. It was the 57th staging of the U.S. National Championships and the fourth Grand Slam tennis event of the year.

Men's Singles Final:

Country	Player	Set 1	Set 2	Set 3	Set 4	Set 5
United States	Don Budge	6	7	6	3	6
Germany	Gottfried von Cramm	1	9	1	6	1

Women's Singles Final:

Country	Player	Set 1	Set 2
Chile	Anita Lizana	6	6
Poland	Jadwiga Jędrzejowska	4	2

Men's Doubles Final:

Country	Players	Set 1	Set 2	Set 3
Germany	Gottfried von Cramm / Henner Henkel	6	7	6
United States	Don Budge / Gene Mako	4	5	4

Women's Doubles Final:

Country	Players	Set 1	Set 2
United States	Sarah Palfrey Cooke / Alice Marble	7	6
United States	Marjorie Gladman Van Ryn / Carolin Babcock	5	4

Mixed Doubles Final:

Country	Players	Set 1	Set 2	Set 3
United States	Sarah Palfrey Cooke / Don Budge	6	8	6
France	Sylvie Jung Henrotin / Yvon Petra	2	10	0

THE COST OF LIVING
COMPARISON CHART

	1937	1937 Price Today (Including Inflation)	2016
House	$8,400	$140,377	$281,800
Annual Income	$1,055	$17,631	$48,187
Car	$1,350	$22,561	$33,560
Gallon of Gasoline	15¢	$2.51	$2.68
Gallon of Milk	18¢	$3.01	$3.86
DC Comic Book	10¢	$1.67	$3.99

BRYLCREEM
THE PERFECT HAIR DRESSING

KEEPS YOUR HAIR IN PERFECT CONDITION

GROCERIES

A&P White Sliced Bread Loaf	5¢
Safeway Butter (per lb)	36¢
Fresh Country Eggs (per dozen)	18¢
Wilsons Lard (4lb carton)	56¢
Granulated Sugar (10lb bag)	49¢
Honey Moon Flour (48 pounds)	$1.29¢
Full Cream Cheese (per lb)	22¢
White House Evaporated Milk (baby size)	7¢
Salt (3x 1½lb boxes)	10¢
Sultana Peanut Butter (quart jar)	25¢
Mello Ripe Bananas (per lb)	4¢
Texas Oranges (per dozen)	19¢
California Lemons (per dozen)	19¢
Strawberries (box)	12½¢
Fresh Florida Tomatoes (lb)	12¢
Hard Head Lettuce (each)	3½¢
New Potatoes (2lb)	13¢
Carrots (2 bunches)	7¢
Home Made Chili (per lb)	15¢
Sliced Cured Ham (per lb)	27¢
Club Steak (2lb)	35¢
Mince Meat (2lbs)	29¢
Salted Mackerel (x2)	25¢
Swift & Co. Sliced Bacon (1lb pkg.)	31¢
Armour's Corned Beef Hash	18¢
Macaroni / Spaghetti (3 boxes)	10¢
Jello (any flavour pkg.)	5¢
Miller's Corn Flakes	10¢
Ginger Ale (per bottle)	10¢
Bokar Coffee (lb)	25¢
Browns Red Seal Asst. Cookies (1lb bag)	23¢
Lux Soap (3 bars)	19¢
Scott Tissue Paper (x3)	20¢

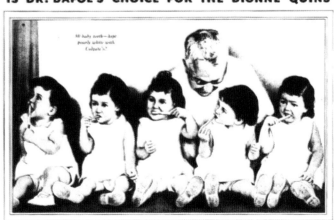
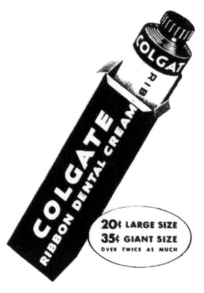

CLOTHES

Women's Clothing

Northmoor Fox Fur Coat	$44.50
Sun Hat	$1.87
Campus Queen Sweater	$1.98
J.M. Dyer Spring Dress	$11.95
Vat Dyed Floral Print Dress	$1.39
Sears Hand Embroidered Night Gown	79¢
Jantzen Swim Suit	$2.95
Austin Quality Shoes	$2.98
Satin Panties & Slip	$1.48
Admiration Stockings (2 pairs)	$1.50

Men's Clothing

Camel's Hair Cloth Polo Coat	$18.50
Gabardine Double Breasted Spring Suit	$20
Marks Bros. Pre-Shrunk Shirt	98¢
Sears Hand Tailored Tie	49¢
Patterned Pyjamas	$1.25
Smooth Horsehide Gloves	$1.49
Leather Belt	75¢
Husky High Cut Leather Boots	$3.49
Work SOX (9 pairs)	88¢

FOUR STAR FEATURE

Sears Sponsor

- Newest Styles
- Latest Patterns
- Smartest Trims
- Finer Fabrics
- Every One Is a Four-Star Feature!

95¢ EACH

THE NEWEST AND PRETTIEST ...THE BIGGEST VALUES, TOO, IN DAYTIME WASH FROCKS!

TOYS

Steelcraft Auburn Pedal Car	$14.95
Deluxe Scooter	$5.49
Redbird Jr. Tricycle	$6.95
Fleet Arrow Sled	$3,49
Lionel Electric Train Set	$9.95
Science Craft Microscope Set	$3.39
Crystal Radio	$1.89
26in Jane Withers Doll	$1.98
Musical Merry-Go-Round	89¢
Baseball Bat, Glove & Ball	69¢
4 Piece Cowboy Set	69¢
Marx G-Man Tommy Gun	94¢
Dad's Big Farm Miniature Farm Machinery	59¢
7 Sanitary Rubber Farm Animals	49¢
7in Adjustable Loom "Learn To Weave"	89¢
Rubber Bricks - Interlocking Building Blocks (296)	$1.89

ELECTRICAL ITEMS

Universal Washer & Wringer	$94
General Electric JB-5 Refrigerator	$164
Westinghouse De Luxe Vacuum Cleaner	$53
Sunbeam Mixmaster Electric Mixer	$38.55
Toastmaster Toaster	$16
Champion Electric Dry Shaver	$9.89
I.E.S. Lounge Lamp	$3.95
Electric Fan	$1.49

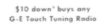

55

OTHER ITEMS

Cadillac Series 60 Touring Sedan	$1660
Cine-Kodak "K" Home Movie Camera	$112.50
¼ Carat Diamond Ring	$39.95
Du Pont Pyralin Dresser Set	$9.69
Plum Tree (3ft)	13¢
Parker Vacumatic Fountain Pen	$5
Sears Bond Street Pipe Set	$1

U.S. COINS

Official Circulated U.S. Coins		Years Produced
Half-Cent	½¢	1792 - 1857
Cent (Penny)	1¢	1793 - Present
2-Cent	2¢	1864 - 1873
3-Cent	3¢	1851 - 1889
Half-Dime	5¢	1792 - 1873
Five Cent Nickel	5¢	1866 - Present
Dime	10¢	1792 - Present
20-Cent	20¢	1875 - 1878
Quarter	25¢	1796 - Present
Half Dollar	50¢	1794 - Present
Dollar Coin	$1	1794 - Present
Quarter Eagle	$2.50	1792 - 1929
Three-Dollar Piece	$3	1854 - 1889
Four-Dollar Piece	$4	1879 - 1880
Half Eagle	$5	1795 – 1929
Commemorative Half Eagle	$5	1980 - Present
Silver Eagle	$1	1986 - Present
Gold Eagle	$5	1986 - Present
Platinum Eagle	$10 - $100	1997 - Present
Double Eagle (Gold)	$20	1849 - 1933
Half Union	$50	1915

CADILLAC leads the *world* in the field above $1500!

Model illustrated—Cadillac Series 60 5-Passenger Touring Sedan, $1660*

 Cadillac sells more cars priced above $1500 than any other motor car manufacturer in the world.

In fact, Cadillac sells almost as many cars in this price field as all the other American manufacturers combined. This has been true for a long time—and it is increasingly true today.

Surely, here is the final proof of how America ranks its motor cars. Seven builders offer cars in this field—and the buyer can take his choice.

Cadillac is made the big favorite for an obvious reason—an unchallenged reputation for prestige, quality and performance.

Always, Cadillac has held to its standards. Not once has its name been given to a car in the lower price range.

Yet, due to advanced manufacturing practice, Cadillac has been able to lower its prices drastically. The Cadillac Series "60" costs approximately half what a Cadillac cost four years ago.

Why not ask your dealer to demonstrate this remarkable car? Learn for yourself why Cadillac leads the world in the quality field!

$1555
AND UP

Delivered price at Detroit, Michigan, subject to change without notice. Prices include all standard accessories. Transportation, State and Local Sales Taxes, Optional Accessories and Equipment—Extra.

58